The course of human evolution has been punctuated by a long succession of chance discoveries and accidental inventions; and in fact, experts estimate that between 30 and 50 percent of all scientific discoveries are in some way accidental.

Think necessity is the mother of invention? Not always. There is a very thin line between brilliant innovation and absolute failure, as some of these inventors famously found out.

Some of the most popular products we use today were accidents stumbled on by clumsy scientists, chefs who spilled things, and misguided inventors who--in the case of the glue used on Post-it Notes--were trying to create the opposite of what they ended up with. But we can all take comfort in knowing even some huge mistakes can come with silver linings, sometimes big enough to change entire industries. And sometimes, even forgetting to wash your hands has its advantages.

The ability to swiftly recognize the utility in something unexpected is one of the profound things that sets us apart from other animals. Whether that's a good thing or not remains to be seen; some serendipitous discoveries have spawned such staggering success that they've become a bit unwieldy.

1. PENICILLIN

Discovered in 1928, Penicillin was one of the world's first antibiotics, but the man who discovered it—**Dr. Alexander Fleming**—never actually meant to "revolutionize all medicine," as he later described it. Rather, Fleming came across the antibiotic entirely by chance when he left out cultures of Staphylococcus aureus in his lab for two weeks and returned to find that their growth had been prevented by a mold called Penicillium notatum.

2. QUININE

Quinine is an anti-malarial compound that originally comes from tree bark. Now we usually find it in tonic water, though it's still used in drugs that treat malaria as well.

Jesuit missionaries in South America used quinine to treat malaria as early as 1600, but legend has it that they heard that it could be used to treat the illness from the native Andean population - and that the original discoverer found these properties with a stroke of luck.

The original tale involved a feverish Andean man lost in the jungle and suffering from malaria. Parched, he drank from a pool of water at the base of a quina-quina tree.

The water's bitter taste made him fear that he'd drank something that would make him sicker, but the opposite happened. His fever abated, and he was able to find his way home and share the story of the curative tree.

This story isn't as well documented as some others, and other accounts for the discovery of quinine's medicinal properties exist, but it's at least an interesting legend of an accidental world-changing finding.

3. SACCHARIN

Saccharin, the artificial sweetener in "Sweet'N Low", is around 400 times sweeter than sugar. It was discovered in 1878 by Constantine Fahlberg, who was actually working an analysis of coal tar at the Johns Hopkins University lab of Ira Remsen.

After a long day in the lab, he forgot to wash his hands before eating dinner. He picked up a roll, and noticed that it seemed sweet - as did everything else he touched.

He went back to the lab and started tasting compounds until he found the results of an experiment combining o-sulfobenzoic acid with phosphorus chloride and ammonia (tasting random chemicals is not generally considered a safe lab practice).

Fahlberg patented saccharin in 1884 (leaving Remsen's name off the patent, despite the fact that they co-published the first paper on the material) and began mass production. The artificial sweetener became widespread when sugar was rationed during World War I.

Tests showed that body couldn't metabolize it, so people didn't get any calories when eating saccharin.

In 1907 diabetics started using the sweetner as a replacement for sugar and it was soon labelled as a noncaloric sweetener (for dieters).

4. VIAGRA

Viagra was the first treatment for erectile dysfunction, but that isn't what it was originally tested for.

Pfizer introduced the chemical Sildenafil, the active drug in Viagra, as a heart medication.

During clinical trials the drug proved ineffective for heart conditions. But men noted that the medication seemed to cause another effect – stronger and longer-lasting erections.

Even if they hadn't been able to maintain an erection before, the ability returned while they were on Viagra.

Pfizer conducted clinical trials on 4,000 men with erectile dysfunction, and saw the same results.

Enter the age of the little blue pill.

5. CORN FLAKES

The recipe for Corn Flakes came out of a botched attempt to cook wheat in 1894.

At that time, John Kellogg was the medical superintendent at Battle Creek Sanitarium, a health facility based on Seventh Day Adventist principles. John and his brother William, who also worked at the sanitarium, were trying to come up with a diet for the patients there.

One day, the brothers put some wheat on to boil, but they accidentally left it cooking too long. When they finally took it off the stove and tried to roll it out into dough, the wheat instead separated into flakes. The brothers discovered they could bake these into a crispy snack.

After some experimentation, they found that the same effect could be achieved using corn instead of wheat, and the recipe for Corn Flakes was born.

6. POST-IT NOTES

You know how when you're done with a Post-it note, you throw it in the wastebasket? Yeah, that was pretty much what Spencer Silver almost did when he was trying to develop a superstrong adhesive for 3M laboratories in 1968 and came up way short. Instead, he had invented the opposite: an adhesive that stuck to objects but could be easily lifted off.

Silver proselytized the potential uses of his new, sort-of-weak glue around 3M for years, all to deaf ears. Finally, a colleague named Art Fry attended one of Silver's seminars in 1974 (3M has long been known for encouraging employees to step outside of their own departments to see what people in other areas of the company are doing). Fry saw a use where no one else did: holding his page in his hymnbook, which his bookmarks kept falling out of. And when you added Silver's mild adhesive to paper bookmarks, a rudimentary Post-it Note was born. Lest you think this is just silly corporate legend, even the Web fact-checker Snopes.com gave this a "True" rating.

3M finally agreed to distribute the Post-it Notes nationwide in 1980, a decade after Silver had first stumbled upon the formula. Thirty years later, they'd be as iconic to the American office as the stapler and the fax machine, with the added bonus of being great for dorm-room pranks and stop-motion animation viral videos.

7. PLASTICS

Can you imagine carrying water bottles made of clay or using disposable utensils made of eggs and animal blood? The legend of the discovery of plastic says that were it not for two accidents, those might be the materials we'd be stuck with today.

The first tale starts in the lab of Charles Goodyear (yes, *that* Goodyear), who combined rubber and sulfur and accidentally put it on the stove for a period of time. When he came back, he found a tough and durable material--created through a process eventually called vulcanization.

The second was a spill in John Wesley Hyatt's shop. Inspired by a $10,000 contest to find a replacement for elephant ivory in billiard balls, Hyatt accidentally spilled a bottle of collodion, only to discover that when it dried it formed a flexible-yet-strong material. He didn't win the contest (nor did anyone, for that matter), but by

1872 his brother Isaiah coined the term *celluloid* to describe what was becoming the first commercially successful plastic--even used in the first motion-picture film used by George Eastman.

8. PACEMAKER

Wilson Greatbatch made a classic dumb move: pulling the wrong part out of a box of equipment. It was a major act of numskullery that became a major part of saving millions of lives.

In 1956, Greatbatch was working on building a heart rhythm recording device at the University of Buffalo. He reached into a box and pulled out a resistor of the wrong size and plugged it into the circuit. When he installed it, he recognized the rhythmic *lub-dub* sound of the human heart. The beat, according to his 2001 obituary in *The New York Times*, reminded him of chats he had had with other scientists about whether an electrical stimulation could make up for a breakdown in the heart's natural beats. Before then, pacemakers were hulking machines the size of TVs. Greatbatch's implantable device of just 2 cubic inches forever changed life expectancy in the world. Now, more than half a million of the devices are implanted every year. Not bad for a numskull.

9. XRAY MACHINE

On November 8, 1895, physicist **Wilhelm Conrad Rontgen** was in his laboratory in Wurzburg, Germany, experimenting on a vacuum tube covered in cardboard when he noticed a mysterious glow emanating from a chemically coated screen nearby. Confused and intrigued, he named the new rays causing this glow *X-rays* due to their unknown origin—and after playing around some more with the new rays, he discovered that putting his hand in front of the glow allowed him to see past his skin to his bones, thus leading to the world's first X-ray.

10. SUPER GLUE

Back in 1942, **Harry Coover** was looking for materials he could use to build clear plastic gun sights for the war, but what he discovered instead was a chemical formulation that stuck to everything it touched. However, his discovery was rejected because researchers didn't see a need for such a sticky formula, and it wasn't until 1951 that the same formula was embraced and repurposed by Coover and fellow Eastman Kodak researcher **Fred Joyner** as "Alcohol-Catalyzed Cyanoacrylate Adhesive Compositions/Superglue," as the patent reads.

11. POTATO CHIPS

Behold the potato chip: the salty, greasy, crispy wisp of tuber for which Americans dole out more than $7 billion a year. The life of the potato chip didn't start out as an accident, more of a prank, but its imminent success took its inventor by surprise. As legend has it, in 1853 Saratoga Springs restaurant cook George "Speck" Crum was annoyed with the complaints of a wealthy patron who repeatedly returned his thickly cut French style potatoes, a common preparation at the time. After the third return, the exasperated Crum sliced the potatoes as thinly as he could, fried the daylights out of them, and covered them in what he assumed to be a prohibitive amount of salt. Much to his surprise, and perhaps initial chagrin, the patron adored them and ordered another round. They quickly became the house specialty, and the history of snacking was changed forever. So much so, in fact, that a major study by Harvard University recently revealed that the potato chip is the number one reason for weight gain in the United States.

(We can't blame Chum for that.)

12. CHAMPAGNE

Because they lived in such high altitudes, the monks of Champagne had plentiful access to all the best grapes. The problem? When the temperatures plummeted in the colder months, the fermentation process on the wine would stop temporarily—and when it began again in the spring, there would be an excess of carbon dioxide inside the wine bottles, which would give the wine unwanted carbonation.

In 1668, the Catholic Church decided that it was time to handle the situation, and so they brought a French monk named **Dom Pierre Perignon** over to Champagne to fix the fermentation problem. However, by the end of the 17th century, people had decided that they actually enjoyed this drink, and Perignon's task thusly changed into making the wine even fizzier. Eventually, Perignon developed the official process for making champagne known as the French Method, crowning him the inventor of the celebratory sip.

13. COCA-COLA

The man who created the syrup for Coca-Cola was not a chef—or even in the food industry. Rather, the soda's inventor was a pharmacist by the name of **Dr. John Stith Pemberton**, who was seeking to create a cocaine- and caffeine-filled alcoholic drink that people with chemical addictions to drugs (including himself) could use to wean off of morphine and other drugs. However, when Prohibition hit, Pemberton was forced to take the alcohol out of his formula (though the cocaine remained for decades), and thus the first bottle of Coca-Cola was made in 1886.

14. SAFETY GLASSES

One fateful day in 1903, scientist **Edward Benedictus** was working in his lab
when he accidentally knocked over a flask. However, when Benedictus looked
down, he noticed that rather than breaking into a million little pieces, the glassware
had actually just cracked slightly while maintaining its shape. After looking into it
a bit further, the scientist learned that what had kept the glass together was
cellulose nitrate coating the inside of the glass—and thusly, safety glass was
created.

15. VELCRO

Swiss engineer George de Mestral was out hunting in the Alps with his dog when
he noticed burrs sticking to its fur. To satisfy his curiosity about what makes burrs
so "sticky", Mestral viewed one under a microscope and observed the tiny hooks
that allow it to latch on to surfaces like fabric and fur. For years, Mestral
experimented with a variety of textiles before arriving at a solution: Velcro, which
he eventually patented. The technology was useful, but really began to take off in
popularity when Apollo astronauts used Velcro to keep objects secure in orbit.

16. TEFLON

Next time you're making breakfast, remember that Roy Plunkett is the reason you're able flip pancake with ease. Long before CFCs became the environmental super-villain depleting the ozone layer, the chemist was aiming to create a new type of chlorofluorocarbon. One day, when Plunkett returned to a refrigeration chamber to check on an experiment, a canister that had contained gas had vanished leaving a few white flakes behind. Upon examining the mysterious substance, he realised it had a very high melting point and was very effective as a lubricant. Teflon was first used in military applications and is now famously applied to cookware around the world.

17. THE ICE CREAM CONE

Today, ice cream fanatics have a choice between enjoying their treat in a cup or a cone, but that wasn't always the case. According to the stories, it wasn't until the 1904 St. Louis World's Fair that someone came up with the idea to spin a wafer-like waffle into the shape of a cone, and this idea was birthed simply out of necessity. When an ice cream vendor at the fair ran out of dishes to serve his ice cream in, the vendor next to him—named **Ernest A. Hamwi**—came up with the idea to shape his waffles into cones as vessels for the frozen treat.

18. VASELINE

In 1859, 22-year-old chemist Robert Chesebrough was investigating an oil well in Pennsylvania when he caught wind of a strange rumour among the oil rig workers: a jelly-like substance known as "rod wax" that constantly got into the machines and caused them to malfunction.

But the substance had a good side, too. Chesebrough noticed that the workers used rod wax to soothe cuts and burns on their skin, and he took some home to experiment with.

The product of his experimentation was what we know today as petroleum jelly, or Vaseline.

19. INSULIN

The discovery that later allowed researchers to find insulin was an accident.

In 1889, two doctors at the University of Strasbourg, Oscar Minkowski and Josef von Mering, were trying to understand how the pancreas affected digestion, so they removed the organ from a healthy dog.

A few days later, they noticed that flies were swarming around the dog's urine - something abnormal, and unexpected.

They tested the urine, and found sugar in it. They realised that by removing the pancreas, they had given the dog diabetes.

Those two never figured out what the pancreas produced that regulated blood sugar. But during a series of experiments that occurred between 1920 and 1922, researchers at the University of Toronto were able to isolate a pancreatic secretion that they called insulin.

Their team was awarded the Nobel prize, and within a year, the pharmaceutical company Eli Lilly was making and selling insulin.

20. VULCANIZED RUBBER

After years of trying to turn rubber into something useful that wouldn't freeze rock hard or melt in the hot sun, Charles Goodyear was struggling.

He'd been experimenting for years and invested everything he owned in rubber research, but hadn't been able to create a commercially viable product, and his family was starving.

But things started to turn around.

First, he poured some nitric acid onto some rubber that had been coloured gold to remove the colour. It turned black, so he threw it out, but removed it from the trash when he realised that it had become hard on the outside, and was smoother and drier than any previous rubber. But it still melted in high heat.

He started using sulphur in his experiments, and here's where things get a little murky. As the story goes, in a fit of excitement, he tossed some rubber that had been treated with sulphur up in the air, and it landed on a stove. But instead of melting, it charred, creating an almost leathery, heat-resistant waterproof substance.

After further experimentation, he realised he could get the most effective results by using steam to heat up the mixture of rubber and sulphur he'd created. Finally, he found success.

Goodyear vehemently disagreed with those who label this finding an accident, since he's the one who followed through with it all. But (if the story is true), the discovery still depended on one lucky accident.

21. MATCHES

Many of us wonder what life was like before electricity or the Internet (shudder), but imagine life before matches. We're talking magnifying glasses and flint. For those of us who like to create controlled flame from time to time with the strike of

a match, we can thank a British pharmacist and his dirty mixing stick. In 1826,
John Walker noticed a dried lump on the end of a stick while he was stirring a mix
of chemicals. When he tried to scrape it off, voila, sparks and flame. Jumping on
the discovery, Walker marketed the first friction matches as "Friction Lights" and
sold them at his pharmacy. The initial matches were made of cardboard but he
soon replaced those with three-inch long hand-cut wooden splints; the matches
came in a box equipped with a piece of sandpaper for striking. Although advised to
patent his invention, he chose not to because he considered the product a benefit to
mankind — which didn't stop others from ripping off the idea and taking over the
market share, leading Walker to stop producing his version.

22. CHOCOLATE CHIP COOKIES

Not all chance discoveries came at the hands of scientists fiddling in labs.
Sometimes they happened to cooks twiddling in kitchens — and sometimes in the
kitchens of restored tollhouses. Case in point: The beloved Toll House Cookie.
Ruth Wakefield and her husband owned and operated the Toll House Inn in
Massachusetts where Ruth cooked for the guests. According to legend, one day in
1937 while making cookie dough, she realized she was out of melting baker's
chocolate and instead used a chocolate bar that she chopped into bits, hoping it

would melt as well. It didn't, and thus was born America's favorite cookie. Did the chocolate chip cookie change the world? Probably not, unless you calculate the combined moments of pleasure derived from biting into one fresh from the oven. They've certainly been responsible for changing a lot of moods.

23. QUININE

Originally found in the bark of the cinchona tree, the discovery of this important anti-malarial compound was a pure accident.

While it was being used by Jesuit missionaries in South America to treat malaria since 1600, they were taught about the substance by native Andean peoples in the first place.

According to their legends, the first discoverer was a feverish Andean man who was lost in the jungle. Suffering from malaria, he drank from a pool of water at the base of a cinchona tree.

Although bitter to the taste, his fever lifted and he survived to pass on what he had learned.

24. THE PURPLE COLOR

In 1856, an 18-year-old student at London's Royal College of Chemistry William Henry Perkin, eager to impress his teacher. His homework assignment was to run experiments at home during the Easter break.

Perkin was tasked with finding a cheap way to produce quinine, a substance used to treat malaria, which had to be extracted from the bark of exotic trees and was thus expensive.

The young man thought he could make it himself in his simple home lab in London. So he started mixing ingredients.

To make artificial quinine, Perkin turned to coal tar, the discarded sludge from Victorian gas lighting. It was believed that the two substances shared a similar chemical structure.

But once he finished his concoction, instead of the normally colorless quinine, all that was left in his test tube was a thick black goo.

When he tried to wash it off, it left behind a vivid purple color. Remarkably, he found that the color transferred to a cloth with untarnished brilliance.

William Henry Perkin had failed to synthesize quinine, but had accidentally invented the first synthetic dye, in one of the most astonishing examples of serendipity in science.

25. CHEWING GUM

Though variations of chewing gum have been around since ancient Greece, the gum that we know today wasn't invented until the late 1800s. It was then that an American inventor named **Thomas Adams, Sr.**, stumbled upon the chewy treat—but only after first trying and failing to turn chicle (the substance that gum is made out of) into rubber.

26. DYNAMITE

Though the explosive substance nitroglycerin was invented by **Ascanio Sobrero**, it was **Alfred Nobel** who used it to make dynamites. While in Paris, Nobel began to experiment with nitroglycerin, and eventually he accidentally found a way to tame the substance by mixing it with *kieselguhr*—though in the process, many people lost their lives, including Nobel's brother Emil.

27. SLINKY

In 1943, naval engineer Richard T. James was working at a shipyard in Philadelphia when he accidentally knocked a spring (that he had been trying to modify into a stabilizer for sensitive maritime equipment) from a high shelf. To his surprise, the spring neatly uncoiled itself and stepped its way down from the shelf and onto a pile of books, and from there onto a tabletop, and then onto the floor. After two years of development, the first batch of 400 "Slinky" toys sold out in just 90 minutes when they were demonstrated in the toy department of a local Gimbels store in 1945.

28. SILLY PUTTY

At the height of World War II, rubber was rationed across the United States after Japan invaded a number of rubber-producing countries across southeast Asia and hampered production. The race was on to find a suitable replacement—a synthetic rubber that could be produced inside the U.S. without the need of overseas imports, which eventually led to the entirely unexpected invention of Silly Putty. There are at least two rival claims to the invention of Silly Putty (chiefly from chemist Earl L. Warrick and Scottish-born engineer James Wright), both of whom found that mixing boric acid with silicone oil produced a stretchy, bouncy rubber-like substance that also had the unusual ability of leaching newspaper print from a page (an ability that changing technology has now eliminated).

ADVICE

THE MISTAKE YOU MAKE TODAY CAN BE ANOTHER NEW INVENTION TOMORROW SO DON'T BE ANGRY AT YOURSELF FOR THAT MISTAKE MADE BECAUSE IT MIGHT JUST BE AN HAPPY MISTAKE.

<u>REFERENCES</u>

Accidental invention -Inc.com

Accidental invention -Businessinsider.com

Accidental invention -Sciencealert.com

Accidental invention -Bestlifeonline.com

www.ingramcontent.com/pod-product-compliance
Lightning Source LLC
Chambersburg PA
CBHW061552250726
48657CB00006B/2463